Poems to Ponder

And Things To Think About!

DALE L. TAYLOR

KITSAP PUBLISHING

POEMS TO PONDER
First edition, published 2018

By Dale L. Taylor

Copyright © 2018, Dale L. Taylor

Cover painting by Elsie Kushner © 2016
Cover painting edited by Kitsap Publishing

Paperback ISBN-13: 978-1-942661-99-3

This is a work of fiction. Names, characters, businesses, places, events and incidents are either the products of the author's imagination or used in a fictitious manner. Any resemblance to actual persons, living or dead, or actual events is purely coincidental.

All rights reserved. No part of this book may be reproduced or transmitted in any form or by any means, electronic or mechanical, including photocopying, recording or by any information storage and retrieval system, without written permission from the author, except for the inclusion of brief quotations in a review.

Published by Kitsap Publishing
P.O. Box 572
Poulsbo, WA 98370
www.KitsapPublishing.com

To my wife, Marilyn, for her love, patience and typing.

"Some say if man were meant to fly, he would have been given wings. I say, if man were meant to follow blindly, without question, he wouldn't have been given a brain."

Dale Taylor

"As a teacher, I am always looking for artistic and original books to share with my students. This book will be read again and again in the classroom. "Poems to Ponder" is a collection of poems that is well written with great care and love for the craft. Younger readers find the poems funny and relatable. For older readers, the poems summon memories of growing up, the importance of family, and a passion for life.

This book will make a nice gift for anyone needing a quick burst of positivity."

~ **Laura Van Amburg**
Educator

"I sat down one winter day and read "Poems to Ponder" from cover to cover, and found myself re-reading some poems again! The poems brought back memories from my childhood to becoming an elder.

Sometimes we get too serious and miss the little things that make life great!!! My students also liked these poems when I read to them."

~ **Dick Krebs**
Retired School Teacher and Coach

"I like these poems because they are more relevant and modern than some. It's nice to read new writers who are captivating and make you think."

~ **Ellen Allmendinger**

"This is so enjoyable! There are lessons to be learned in these poems. Everyone should read this book."

~ **Lila Eubanks**
Artist

"I loved *"Poems to Ponder"*. They brought back so many memories and took me back to my youth, read it. You'll see what I mean!"

~ **Sharon Six**

Table of Contents

We Men Just Don't Understand	1
Perspective	3
Monogamy	5
Miracles	6
The Little Miracle Church in Old Santa Fe	7
A Wonderful World of White	9
Now I Lay Me Down	10
Is It Reasonable	11
A Few Simple Pleasures	12
To Soar with Wings	14
Dare To Be First	15
Rare Is the One Who Stays	16
When Everything Was New	17
Zero Degrees of Separation	18
It's Been Fun, But It's Over	20
Paradise, For Some	22
Different Is Good	24
One Day In Mexico	25
Make Memories	28
To Believe Or Not Does It Matter?	29
After The Baby Bump	30
The Beginning, The In-Between, and The End	32
This Word Love	33
Mysterious Waters	34
Harvey	36
Clouds	38
My First Car	39
The Moods of Neptune	40
The Sound Of Silence	41
Time Through Different Eyes	42
Shadows of The Past	43
The New Me	44
Playtime in The Ocean	45
You Can't Go Back	47
Water's Journey	49
An Ode to My Commode	50
Dad's Gone	52
Mother's Gone	53
Think It Through	54
"To Sleep, Perchance To Dream"	55
My Folks	57
What Goes Around……….	59
End of The Line In Socorro	60
Caught in the Middle	62
Turning Points	63
Lovely Wings	64
Our Real Heroes	66
Go Fish	67
Procreation In Gooseville: A Love Story	68
The Person Within	70
Tough Ole Birds	71
Kiss the Blarney Stone	73
My Buddy, My Beer and My Boat	75
North to Alaska	76
The Wind and The Palm	77
Watermelon Boy	78
Now Is The Time	79
It's A Different World Today	80
Sept. 11, 2001 Another day in infamy	81

We Men Just Don't Understand

I've tried to write from a woman's view
but finally decided that I no can do.
I just don't understand how they think.

Two or three hours in a grocery store
when the things she needed were only three or four.
What in the world can she be doing for all that time?

Read the label one line at a time
to make sure the ingredients are all just fine.
Please, just put it in the cart and let's go home.

Driving down the road at fifty miles an hour
she screams, "Yard sale, let's stop for a while."
I slam on the brakes and lose an inch of rubber.

Another hour of my life lost
looking for things at a low, low cost
that will go in our own yard sale later on.

Going on a trip. In two days we'll be back.
How can it take her three days to pack?
Just throw in an extra shirt for me. I'm good to go.

Clothes and shoes, shoes and clothes.
It's a never ending search, God knows.
How can anyone spend so much time on
what to wear.

She speaks woman. I speak man.
I need an interpreter to understand
most of what she is trying to say.

Continued on the next page

Refrigerator and two freezers full of food,
enough for twenty years or more,
and she's still clipping coupons from
the local grocery store.

And women are worriers, that's for sure,
something bad's always about to occur.
That's why we men have to be strong.

But if they were the opposite of what they are now
we wouldn't like it anyhow.
We might complain and gripe and make a fuss,
but if they weren't them.....
they would be us!

Perspective

When I look around at our world it's easy to see
how important we, as humans, must be.
Like little gods, above other living things
because we can imagine,
and with that, the entitlement it brings.

We wonder why things are as they are,
why we are here and ponder the stars.
A human mind is a wonderful thing
its ability to create and the joys it can bring.
But it also brings questions without easy answers.
How to end war, how to cure cancer.

If everyone put their energy, into problems that are real,
instead of fighting over things ethereal,
just think what a great world this could be
if everyone thought in terms of you and me,
working together to bring out the best
to make a good life and forget all the rest.

Suppose we look at our planet in a different way
from far, far above, we'd look down and say,
"What a tiny little speck I see
in the dark vastness of our galaxy."

Only one tiny, pinpoint of light
like billions of others that sparkle in the night,
not the huge place it seems to us humans,
that inspires this feeling of importance within us.

We're like microbes on a little ball
no more or less important than any or all
of the untold billions of planets,
that hang in the sky.
The only difference being,
we can wonder why?

Monogamy

If you observe the animal world
take note and you will find,
that devotion to just one mate is rare
no matter what the kind.

The male is usually solitary
roaming to and fro
until a female decides the time is right
and gives the word to go.

The same holds true, for the most part,
in the world of human beings,
although we try, to deny,
the similarity that exits between.

We try to fight the urges
that are so strong when we are young
and can cause so many problems
until finally they are gone.

It's much easier to be monogamous
when the years have made you old,
and when the most important thing is
someone you love to snuggle with to
keep from getting cold.

Miracles

"It's a miracle," we often hear people say.
but could it be just something,
we don't understand today?

There are so many things now common to us
that would have been miracles before,
but our knowledge at that time
was so far behind,
and today we know so much more

But we don't know it all
and we never will.
So when the unexplained happens to us,
until we find out
what it's all about,
it will still be a 'miracle,' I guess.

Then, there are the other kind of 'miracles,'
the kind that can't be true,
that are more like magician's tricks
to create wonder in me and you.

But there are those who still insist
that these 'miracles' they must believe,
somehow in order to bolster their faith
but could it be they're just naive?

The Little Miracle Church in Old Santa Fe

In a place called Santa Fe, a little town down
New Mexico way,
a church was built to serve the town
and people to come from miles around.
But when it was built they forgot
to think of a way to get to the loft.
A place for the choir was needed up there,
but the room was too narrow for conventional stairs.

They called in professionals to study the problem,
but none could come up with a solution to help them.
With nowhere to turn, the nuns started to pray,
for God to help them, to show them the way.

Shortly thereafter a stranger appeared, leading a
donkey carrying all of his gear.
"I'm a carpenter by trade," the stranger professed.
"I'll look at your problem and give it my best."

He worked by himself and when he was through,
he had built something wonderful, something brand new.
A spiral staircase with no center pole prop.
It was only attached at the bottom and the top.

The nuns were amazed at what he had done
and set out to thank him for being the one
that answered their prayers, but found he had left,
leaving behind his wonderful gift.

Where he came from, where he went to,
I don't know if the story is true,
but the church still stands in old Santa Fe
and if you go there you'll see it today.

Loretto Chapel - Photos by Blue Rose Photography.

A Wonderful World of White

Snow flakes,
slowly, slowly, drifting down
like a billion tiny, white
feathers softly, quietly to the ground.
Each one unlike no other,
fingerprints in frozen water.

As time goes by
snow covers the ground,
eventually turning everything around,
into a beautifully, clean, wonderful place,
for now, nothing dirty to mar its face.

Moonlight glistens
off the white covered grass
like acres and acres
of small shards of glass.

Soon, children rush out to start their day
in this wonderland of white to play,
in forts and tunnels with snow balls to throw,
snowmen to build and angels of snow.

It won't take long for the
whiteness to change,
to something less clean,
less beautifully maintained.

But as we see this change
in our hearts we all know,
it'll be beautiful again
with the very next snow.

Now I Lay Me Down

A cemetery.
A garden of granite flowers.

The tips of monoliths poking up from
beneath the earth, to pay tribute
to the people lay resting
forever under the soft green
carpet, that separates them
from the darkness of forever
and the brightness of the world
of the living,
that they'll never see again.

They live only in the memories
of their friends and families left behind,
but with each passing generation
the thoughts and memories of those
gone before, become fewer and fewer
until all that remains are some old,
faded photographs of people no longer known,
and the engravings on a tombstone.

So I will try, as should you, to create
something in my life, that will be cherished
by the ones I will leave behind
when my final day comes.

I do not fear death.
I only regret the permanence of it
and all of the things to come,
that I will not be there to see.

Is It Reasonable

The most wonderful gift we've been given
is the ability to reason.
By not using reason and
logic, we are like blind men
following the politician,
priest, or con man,
who is the most skillful
at telling us what we want to hear.

And we all want to hear
what we want to hear.
So we search out that person
who claims to know what we do not.

And it doesn't matter if he knows or not.
It only matters if we believe or not.
We give him the power over our lives
by our trust and belief in what he professes.

Blind faith only creates blind men,
like sheep following aimlessly behind,
being led to whatever their leader dictates,
for whatever reasons he desires.

Faith sounds good
but should never be a substitute for
reason, logic and proof.

A Few Simple Pleasures

Walking barefoot in the sand at the
edge of a vast ocean while the breezes
coat your skin with salt spray and shore
birds dart this way and that in search
of tiny morsels hidden away in the surf
that rolls in and out gently over your feet.

Moving your tongue round and round on
a delicious, sweet ice cream cone on a
hot, summer day, while sweat beads on
your forehead, and ice cream drips
unknowingly from the little hole in the
bottom of the cone onto your lap.

Lying on a blanket, in a field of flowers
in the mountains,
basking in the after-glow of love making,
and later at home, searching each other for ticks.

Holding a beautiful rose to your face,
after the thorns have been stripped from
the stem, and feeling the soft, velvety,
petals tickle your nose, as you breathe
in the wonderful essence that only a
fragrant rose can produce.

Lying in a soft, warm bed in the early morning,
trying to squeeze in another hour of sleep,
while a morning dove outside your window
coo-coo's for its mate, over and over and over and over......

Picking a small, crying baby from its crib
and holding it gently to your shoulder,
and feeling the sobs slowly subside into little
gasps as it falls asleep against your cheek,
feeling safe and secure in your arms.

Trying new foods from far-a-way lands
that you will never get to visit.

Sunrises, sunsets, rainstorms, lightning shows.
Mother Nature's ever-changing beauty.

Watching your children, grandchildren, great grandchildren grow,
in the knowledge that your lineage will live on.

To Soar with Wings

Do you ever wonder what it would be like to fly like a bird?
I do!

To float for hours on the wind currents over
the ocean with almost no effort, like a frigate bird.

Or skim the surface like a pelican
barely an inch above the waves,
never touching the water.

Maybe a hawk circling a half mile in the sky
searching with binocular eyes
for a tasty morsel far, far below.

To be a humming bird hovering in the air
like a tiny helicopter searching for an enemy
that hides within the blossoms
of a honeysuckle plant.

A seagull as it dives headlong into the water
at the speed of a missile,
somehow, without breaking its neck.

How incredible it must be to fly!

But then, I return from my reverie
and embrace the reality.

I cannot flap my arms hard enough to leave the ground.
The wind in my face makes my eyes water
and my tail has no feathers.

But I guess being earth-bound
isn't quite so bad after all.

Dare To Be First

They lay there in the dark, damp soil
waiting patiently for the sun above to
melt away most of the snow that
still lay covering the roof overhead.

Finally, the earthen barrier was sufficiently
warmed and they slowly push upwards,
first breaking through the soil that had
held them captive in the dark for so long,
then with extra effort, breached the soft,
cold layer of snow that was all that remained
of winter's presence.

Finally, into the warm rays of the sun,
emerged the most daring, adventurous,
excited to be the first of its kind,
to announce that spring has arrived.

The crocus! What a brave little flower!

Others wait until they are sure that winter
threatens no more before daring to show
their beauty to the world, but the crocus,
maybe with a 'little man complex' always
dares to be first.

Rare Is the One Who Stays

Acquaintances are many.
True friends are few.
The ones who care the most
stay with you,
no matter what you do.

Of all the people that you meet
in your journey through your life,
there may be only one or two
who stay with you
through good and strife.

Most are close
when everything is fair,
but if things go wrong,
feelings get hurt,
it's rare to find them there.

So if you're lucky
to have that one or two,
value them as you would gold,
and constantly renew.

When Everything Was New

It's a shame that as the years accumulate
and our minds are filled with more and more
of the mundane goings on of our everyday
lives, that we can't remember our earliest
years, when every small thing was
a new and exciting adventure.

Nothing had yet been experienced.
Wouldn't it be wonderful to feel anew the
sense of accomplishment in our first steps or the
warmth and safety at being held close to our
parents' breasts. Our first taste of ice cream.

When even the tiniest of things was of profound
interest and deserving of intense scrutiny.
A baby studying the every movement of an ant.

What a glorious and exhilarating time that has
been erased from our memories.
The years before we became burdened, and
blessed, with the responsibilities of growing
toward adulthood.

The years that somehow never became
imprinted in our memory bank.
So many firsts forgotten.

The lost years!

Zero Degrees of Separation

The one thing other than power and greed
that makes men fight for what they think they need,
are the labels we put upon our selves
that separate us from everyone else.

This separation between us could imply,
that the differences between you and I
are so vast and have gone on so long
because, I am right and you are wrong.

Even if we believe this is true,
maybe no one is right, neither me nor you.
But we'll fight to the death to defend our beliefs.
Bring those other labels down to their knees.

Catholic or Muslim, Christian or Jew,
killed by the millions because each knew
only their belief could be the true one.
All can't be right, but all could be wrong
and the horrors committed can't be undone.

I know we'll never put labels aside
because most of us just can't abide
to be left out, not part of a group,
on our own, out of the loop.

We want to feel like we belong
to something larger, something strong.
Be it political party, club or team,
belonging to something is part of our scheme.
I guess labels will always be part of our
lives, to tell one group from another
but must we despise
those that think other than you and me.
Must we kill because we think differently?

Will there be a time with differences so few
that labels will mean nothing to me and you,
when people get along and live together in peace?
PROBABLY NOT!!

It's Been Fun, But It's Over

There used to be little Molly.
The girl that would lay next to me on the couch
while we watched TV until her restlessness
overcame her and she had to find an outlet
for her stored up energy.

That's when it would start.

First, maybe with her messing up my hair.
Then the pinching of my nose or bending my fingers.
We would then end up on the floor wrestling,
with me tickling her until she was close
to wetting her pants.

And there were always lots of hugs and kisses.
Back when little Molly really liked her grandpa.

But, time stands still for no one.
Little Molly became big Molly, a teenager!

Her world changed, our world changed.
She no longer needed a babysitter, so
the sleepovers virtually stopped.

Visits became almost non-existent except
when granddaughter and mother came to pick up
grandmother to go shopping or to lunch
for a ladies' day out.

These brief stops usually consist of
time for some M&M's from the candy
bowl and maybe a "hello" and "goodbye grandpa."

But, she's living in a woman's world now.
Just put grandpa on an ice floe and
push him out to sea. No longer needed!

Big Molly is a great young lady
But I sure miss little Molly.

Paradise, For Some

Close your eyes and picture this scene.
You're way down south and living a dream
on a beach in old Mexico, sun in your face
feeling the soft breezes blow,
laying on a blanket with feet in the sand.
On the air drifts the music of a mariachi band.

The pelicans and gulls are filling the air
circling and diving, fighting for a share
of the morsels of food that swim there below,
or maybe some tidbits the humans might throw.

The beautiful brown children, some naked as can be,
run laughing and calling and splashing in the sea,
while fathers drink beer and laugh at their jokes
and mothers watch the kids and fix lunch for the folks.

With cold drink in your hand you start thinking of food,
and on the breeze comes the smell of something real good.
The delicious aroma of tacos and meat
and the grilling of shrimp makes you jump to your feet.

Later that day as you walk through the town
joining other tourists and gazing around
at the myriad of shops selling trinkets and gifts,
you may think to yourself "what a paradise this is."

But if you take the time to leave the main street,
you may discover what most tourists don't see.
The same people who sell you the gifts and the food
make beautiful music so your time there is good,
may go back to their homes of cardboard and wood.
Some with dirt floors and six to a room,
still try to stay clean, sweep the dirt with a broom.

- Poem continued on next page -

Put yourself in their place. Try if you can!
Work like a dog, still can't feed the kids.
Misery for the wife. Hard to feel like a man.

So the next time you enjoy your time at the beach
in some tropical land you can afford to reach,
Think about why those people leave, their country, their home
The 'paradise' that we perceive.

Different Is Good

The differences in some people are obvious to see.
We know they look different, than you and me.
The color of their skin, their eyes and their hair.
The way that they speak and the clothes that they wear.

They may come from a part of the world we don't know,
to us, strange and exotic, but to them, not so.
Customs so strange, as ours are to them
but wouldn't it be dull if we all were the same?

We feel comfortable and safe, with our own kind
and may be fearful and suspicious of those that we find
so unlike what we're used to, until we can see,
with an effort to know them, they're like you and me.

Try to look past the color of the skin
and take time to learn of the person within.
You may find that the differences we see
are not as important as the sameness can be.

To be safe and secure, a place to call home,
family and friends, maybe a car that we own.
Good health, long life, children to rear.
These are the things that we all hold so dear.

So don't judge so fast, the people you see,
who don't look or sound just like you and me.
Appreciate the diversity these cultures they bring,
to fight against monotony, make our lives interesting.

Would you want a world where we all look the same?
Speak the same language. Wouldn't that be a shame?
Wear similar clothes, eat the same food,
same art, same music.   No! Different is good!

One Day In Mexico

It's a crisp, chilly morning, still mostly dark,
as we slide our boat into the waters of
San Lucas cove, in Baja, California.

With a hard tug on the lanyard the
mercury outboard fires up and we slowly
move out.

On either side, sting rays dart away in the
shallow water like gray birds scattering
from the disturbance we're causing.

We pick up speed and slice through the
water, throwing up a rooster-tail in our
wake as we make the turn around the
break water and enter the Sea of Cortez.

What a glorious morning it is as the
red sun peeks over the ridge of San Marcos
Island five miles in the distance.

We turn and run full speed to the area
where we hope to find our quarry.
Up and down, riding the swells as one
would ride a horse, like a cowboy of the sea.

Finally, we're on the hunt, pulling
plastic lures fifty feet behind at eight
miles an hour, skipping off the water
in imitation of flying fishes.

On and on, time goes by, until suddenly
the pole bends violently and the reel
screams in pain as the line peels off
at an unbelievable speed.

Continued on the next page

Behind us the bright golden fighting
colors of a great dolphin fish, or
Dorado, as it is known in Mexico, leaps high
and thrashes in a valiant effort to
rid itself of the hook imbedded in its mouth.

Several times the great fish is brought
near the boat only to explode away again
at the sight of the gaff.

But, eventually he tires and the gaff
strikes home and he's brought into the boat.
He looks at us through eyes as big as quarters,
almost human, as his life fades and the beautiful
golden color turns quickly to not so beautiful
gray-green. What a thrilling, yet sad, moment.

Fishing time over, we start our way home.

The water has changed from choppy to a thick,
flat, eerie, gray, silvery color. So mysterious and
spooky you almost expect a giant tentacle
to come over the side and wrap around you,
and pull you into the deep.

Seagulls are following and pelicans glide
effortlessly inches above the water and tiny
Grebes, like baby ducks, dive as we pass by.

The day is over. The fish are cleaned.
and we are happy.

As they say, "a bad day of fishing is better
than a good day at work."

Author with nice Dorado (Mahi Mahi) in Mexico.

Make Memories

Every road we go down,

Every path that we walk,

Every person we meet,

Every mistake that we make,

Every new place that we see,

adds a small piece to the storehouse

of experience that we tuck away, deep inside,

to recover in our later years,

to re-live in our memories,

until with time, even those begin to fade away

like smoke drifting up to disappear in the heavens.

To Believe Or Not Does It Matter?

If heaven really is a place
and eternity is what we all face,
I wonder what it could be
to make some so anxious to see.

Can it be everything to everyone
depending on what they sought,
or one universal truth,
and what they want, matters naught.

Some may believe in streets of gold
and angels playing harps,
but these are scenes from painter's brushes.
That's where they got their start.

There are men that can't wait to die
to get their seventy virgins.
I wonder what the women get
some men that don't deserve them?

Do people really think about
the things that they believe,
or just accept what others say?
They must know more than me!

I believe in nature's ways
that's all that really matters,
not god's, or devils, witches and such
or Alice and the Madhatter.

The Easter Bunny and Santa Claus
were our heroes when we were small,
but when we grew, that's when we knew,
they didn't exist at all.

As adults we have the same doubts and fears
as we had in our younger years.
So I believe, we create, new heroes
in a supernatural state.

Bigger, stronger, smarter than we,
it doesn't matter that those we can't see,
it only matters, I guess, as it should,
that believing like this
makes people feel good.

After The Baby Bump

Is there anything more beautiful
or joyful to behold
than that of a newborn baby
come into this bright, new world.

To cradle this amazing being
that you've helped bring to life
and gaze into that chubby face
born of the love of a husband and wife.

Now it's gurgling and cooing
peeing and pooing.
Diaper changing that never stops.
But it all seems worthwhile
when that baby smiles,
and you feel so proud you could pop.

You wouldn't trade those years
for anything in the world,
the happiness in raising a boy or a girl.
But when you think back, how it was then,
you probably say to yourself
"I wish they were little again."

The Beginning, The In-Between, and The End

First, there was nothing,

then there was life.
The beginning of years
full of happiness and strife.

We start out as babies
then grow to our teens.
As yet too young
to know what life means.

Later into our lives comes
someone to share,
all the hopes and dreams
with a partner who cares.

We work at our jobs
doing our best to
succeed, so that we can acquire
all the things that we need.

The children come along
and too soon they all leave
to start their adult lives
on their own as did we.

With hope in our hearts
we pray as they go,
that we did enough
so they'll need us no more.

The years pass by quickly.
The hair turns to gray.
Our friends and our kin
have all passed away.

Our muscles are withered.
Our eyesight is bad.
Our hearing and memory
is not like we had.

Soon the end will come
and as I said at the start.
It'll end as it began
As------nothing.

This Word Love

Is there a word with more meanings
than this word love?
There must be as many
as stars up above.

We love our car
we love our house,
we love our shoes,
we love our spouse.

We love this food
and we love that.
The color blue
and our new hat.

The speaker loves
that he is here
and loves the audience
that sits so near.

We love the weather
and love our pet.
Some love to gamble
can't wait to bet.

I love you
and you love me
although each other
we rarely see.

But never seem
to care enough
to find the time
to keep in touch.

Love is a word
that's overused,
and in relationships
sometimes abused.

So when you say
"I love my bike,"
the word you really mean
is 'like'.

So think about this word we use
and toss about so freely.
Maybe if we used it less
it would come to have more
meaning.

Mysterious Waters

A person can spend hours and hours
walking by the edge of the sea.
Sunrises, sunsets, reflecting on water
waves rolling in so care-free.

Constantly changing, never the same,
soothing, yet mysterious and dark.
It has this strange pull, you want to go in,
but in the back of your mind you think, 'shark'!

There's so much life that exists in these waters
the dangerous, lovely and strange.
A myriad of creatures, too numerous to count
and many yet unknown and un-named.

We know more of the moon and some of the planets,
then what lives deep down below.
What alien life, weird and bizarre
mankind is dying to know.

But for me, I'm content, to fish from a boat
catching whatever I can,
or stroll on the beach, searching for shells
and enjoying my feet in the sand.

There's so much to find, new things to discover
that wash up from the waters below,
when storms blow up and waves come crashing
and toss their treasures to and fro.

If you have patience and look carefully,
who knows what you might find,
a seahorse or starfish dried in the sun
or sea glass if you're so inclined.

The ocean can be whatever you want
for relaxing or adventures galore.
But, for all we know of these wondrous depths
someday we'll know so much more.

Harvey

The monster crept slowly along
far out in the mid-Atlantic,
it's winds swirling madly,
the waters churning and frantic.

As it moved north, became larger and larger,
it grew to incredible size.
And nowhere within this terrible beast
was there room for compromise.

The people of Texas knew this was bad.
On this they could all agree.
And as they awaited what was to come
they named the monster 'Harvey'.

This is the one that only comes along
maybe once in a thousand years,
leaving in its wake, death and destruction
and rivers and rivers of tears.

The winds blew hard and it was bad
but the rains it brought were worse,
measured no more in inches, but feet,
everything it sought to immerse.

It lingered over the state
'til it decided to leave,
but then returned once more.
It seemed there was no reprieve.

At last the behemoth moved away
to share its terror with others,
leaving behind in the wreckage and ruin,
death, and the wailing of mothers.

Big trucks, boats, and rubber floats
rescuing those from waist deep water.
People on roof tops waving their arms,
waiting under 'copters that hover.

Strangers helping those in need
where all their belongings were lost,
regardless of race, color or creed,
not thinking of the time or cost.

We think of heroes in times of war
doing daring and incredible feats,
but there are thousands more in days like these
who jump in to help in a heart-beat.

We always come back from things like this
because we know how to cope.
And when we see how others pitch in,
in our hearts we know there is hope.

Clouds

When I gaze into the clouds I see
a whole new world open up to me.

Miles of fluffy, cotton balls
that slowly change until they're all
something different than they've been
and never to be the same again.

I see a rabbit, now a dog, no, wait,
it's changed into a frog.
Castles, dragons, faces and such,
it's hard to believe you can see so much.

If you just take some time to lay in the grass
and look to the sky with wonder and ask,
"What lies hidden in these amorphous things
that only with imagination can bring
anything your mind can see."
What a wondrous thing
a cloud can be

My First Car

I fondly remember my first car.
Well, maybe fondly isn't quite the right word.

I was in my teens and I was desperate to own a
ride. You know, for freedom, and of
course, girls.

And I was automobile illiterate.
Not mechanically inclined.
Change oil, plugs. That's about it!
And not much money.

Went car shopping with dad. Found one that
I liked. Dad said, "no," wasn't any good,
but it was cute and only a hundred and ten dollars.
I bought it. What did dad know anyway.

That cute car didn't run for a week.
Funny, don't even remember what happened to it.

Should have listened to my dad!!!

The Moods of Neptune

The ocean's waters sit quietly as though resting,
moving gently upon the shore with almost loving
strokes, caressing the land like a mother would
her child.

Then, with the help of the wind and the moon,
the waters build, slowly at first, until
the waves beat harder and faster upon the land
as though it's only purpose is to turn boulders
into fine grains of sand.

Crashing over and over into rocks and bluffs,
throwing flotsam and spraying phosphorescence into
the air as if a miniature Fourth of July celebration.

Skies darken, thunder smashes down like rocks
being thrown from the heavens and lightning
splits the skies above like knife slashes in the dark.

And the waves beat on and on, relentlessly,
slowly wearing away the wall that stands in its way.

Unlike humans, who invented time to measure
their meager lifespans, time has no meaning to
these elements. They just are!
Interacting endlessly, over and over, like these waters,
in a dance without end.

Then slowly, everything begins to change again.

The air above quiets.
The winds calm and the waves become
smaller and smaller until this liquid giant
once again sleeps peacefully until it decides
to resume it's never ending battle with
the shoreline that restrains it.

The Sound Of Silence

Some feel the need to constantly fill the
air with a never-ending stream of syllables
and consonants and nouns and adjectives
as though something bad might happen
if there's a pause in the flow of words.

Like those who must fill every inch of a wall
with knick-knacks and pictures because they feel an
empty space should always be filled with something.

But, really, silence is good!

It gives the mind time to sort through things.
Separate the good from the bad,
necessary from unnecessary,
decipher what's been said,
plan for what's to come.

The time in bed, in the darkness, before going to sleep,
and in the morning after we awake,
and lay there in the silence with only our thoughts,
before rising to start the day,
is a wonderful, soothing, experience to be enjoyed
fully before being subjected to the litany of sounds
and distractions that await us.

An escape from the people, cars, horns, barking dogs, planes,
sirens and televisions of virtually every waking moment
of our lives.
Yes, silence is a very good thing!

Time Through Different Eyes

Funny, the different speeds at which time moves.

The pace of a turtle crawling through mud

when you're young and looking forward to the future,

and the speed of a bullet train when looking

back to the past.

One day you're a kid with everything ahead,

then in a flash you're an old, Monday morning

quarterback thinking, "coulda, woulda,

shoulda," about the life already spent.

Shadows of The Past

Each of us lives in the shadows

of those that have come before.

Some that we've known,

but most we have not.

But each of those long gone

have contributed a little

to what we are today,

just as we, sometimes unknowingly,

are doing the same

for those we will leave behind

to walk in our shadows.

The New Me

As I look in the mirror
what do I see,
a little old man
looking back at me.

Not the virile young man
I knew in my youth,
but someone quite different,
getting long in the tooth.

I remember quite clearly
when those days I would
boast, of the many times spent
sowing wild oats.

This body could run
for miles and miles
and from the girls
elicit their smiles.

How it has changed.
Not for the better, instead,
now I get tired
just getting out of bed.

Skin once so clear
now it is not.
I challenge Dalmatians
for the number of spots.

Getting up from the floor
my knees they do creak,
and twelve times a day
I have to go pee.

The doctor says "watch it,
and don't overdo.
And, by the way,
here's more medicine for you."

So take note of these words
to you I do speak.
For sure, getting old
is not for the weak.

Playtime in The Ocean

Have you ever watched whales
in their watery world
gliding along,
hardly making a swirl?

A cow with her calf
swimming close by.
The mother protective
keeping an eye.

Then out of the blue
coming straight up
like a marine missile
shot from a gun,

comes Moby Dick
showing panache,
falling back down
with a mountainous splash.

A huge flipper slams
hard on the water,
loud as a rifle shot
to signal the others.

Whales at play.
What a marvelous display
of these gentle beings
in a giant's ballet.

To be near these behemoths
and see them close by
is a wonderful thrill,
like a spiritual high.-

You Can't Go Back

They say you can't go back,
but I did!

Back to where I spent my youth.

Back to the gravel road and the quarter acre
lot with the out-house at the far end.

Time reverses itself and once again I'm that
boy, very small, running and hiding with my brother
in this huge playground that was our home.

Raising rabbits, chasing chickens, playing hide and
seek and eenie einie over.

I can hear my mother calling for my brother and
me to come in for supper.

Bathing in a galvanized tub of water on the
kitchen floor next to the wood stove where we
cooked and heated our water.

I can taste the first sip of whiskey that my father
had me try to satisfy my curiosity and to discourage
future use. It worked! The burning in my throat
sent me running to the water bucket on the kitchen counter.

I'm watching, and trying in my small way, to help
my father and his father build this huge garage
to shelter our old, square, Pontiac car.
I hear this loud, heart wrenching howl
coming from outside. It's my father having trouble
cutting the tail off a new pup.

Continued on the next page

Here I am, waiting patiently under a bushy
tree, holding my BB gun tightly in my hands
and hoping that I won't miss with my first
shot, and with that, become the victim myself
in this hunt for the terrible, ferocious,
sharp-beaked, fluffy, feathered sparrow.

Now it's winter and the snow is deep and
we love it. Time for forts and piles of snow balls
for our wars. Who can build the biggest snowman.
Galoshes with metal snaps. Mittens and gloves
soaked through till our fingers, turned to icicles,
force us to run indoors and huddle around the
"Spark" oil heater to thaw out.

All these memories come flooding back, almost
like my life repeating itself.

Then I look again.

The street has been paved. The outhouse is gone.
The huge garage is just a small one car shed.
The yard that seemed liked acres and acres made
for adventures is much smaller.

Everything seems much smaller than it was back then.

Who says you can't go back?
Of course you can!

But it's just never the same!

Water's Journey

Do you ever watch a river flow
and wonder just what makes it go?
You'd think that someday it would
stop, run out of water at the top.

But raindrops fall and snow melts down,
adding moisture to the ground.

Moisture turns to rivulets small
and millions add to streams that fall,
down mountain sides and grassy field,
nothing in the way to cause it to yield.
Finally, as we all know,
they come together in the river's flow.

There, sometimes slowly, sometimes fast,
we watch the waters rushing past
inexorably to the ocean,
to once again, through nature's whim,
set the return trip in motion.

An Ode to My Commode

If there's one place
a man can go
to spend some time
and be all alone, it's
that little room
at the end of the hall.
The little room
with the porcelain throne.

It's peaceful and quiet
and so serene,
with the smell of the Clorox
that makes it so clean

The lighting is good
so if I need
I can see all the things
that I'd like to read.

Just to sit here and bask
in this time, all alone,
till my wife finally asks
why I'm taking so long.

When I've done
what I've come here to do
and I'm feeling so good
when the process is through

I press the lever
to activate the flush.
In comes the water
and disappears in a rush.

What a feeling of power
to create this cyclone
in your own little kingdom
with its porcelain throne.

Dad's Gone

Asthma
Emphysema

The two things my father had to live with. No choice with the asthma.
The emphysema was another matter.
Just one of the gifts bestowed upon him by this demon called nicotine.

After a life time of smoking he quit. Cold turkey!
It was already too late!

The heartache of watching him give up the things he most liked to do.

Trips to the hospital where nothing meaningful could be done.

My mother's tears time and time again.
Two years on oxygen to try to prolong the inevitable.

His saying that he was no good to anyone. Helpless, why not just die.

No appetite. Wasting away. Thin. Bed sores. Memory gone.

Then 7:00 one morning, a call came from mom.
She heard him take his last breath in the middle of the night.

He's no longer suffering.

Mother's Gone

Here we are the two of us, in this hospital room together. My mother brought here from the nursing home, and me, her middle son, trying to convey the love and appreciation I feel for her, but not knowing if she's even aware. She has severe osteoporosis and she's dehydrated, but that's not all! The doctor says she has bone cancer. She's 82 years old and ready to go, but doesn't know her time is so near.

The doctor gives her maybe a week. How can this be?
This woman has been here all of my life.
It's the third day here.
She isn't responding now and I sense the end is at hand.

I call my older brother and tell him to hurry, but before he arrives
she gasps for breath twice and she's gone.
I'm still holding her hand.

Now he's here and I hold him tight as he cries in my arms.

Sometimes it's hard to be the strong one

Think It Through

Do you think, do you ask,
do you question those,
who profess a knowledge of things unknown,
that only a few can understand,
and with that knowledge keep the rest in hand.

It's easy to concede,
our power of rational thinking,
give the power over to others
and let them do the leading.

If things are said that sound too bizarre,
and stories told that go too far,
ask yourself, can this really be right,
or designed to fill us with wonder or fright,

to make us believe in things not true
so the power stays with them,
not me and not you.

If stories are old, and told and retold,
they might not always be true,
might just only be old.
And just because those men are dead,
don't believe everything they've said.

Just use your brain
and your power to reason.
If it doesn't make sense
it's nothing to believe in.

"To Sleep, Perchance To Dream"

Sleep.

What a curious thing it is to sleep.
To voluntarily opt out of life for eight hours
or so everyday.

To teach our babies to recite, before going to bed, things like,
"If I should die before I awake." How scary!

We lay there with eyes closed, trying to will ourselves
into the blackness of sleep, while a thousand random
thoughts run in and out, pushing against the veil
of darkness that we seek.

Then we enter that area of la la land, where
full sleep has not been attained, but we
are still semi-conscious of things around us---
and time slips by.

And the dreams come!
Crazy dreams!
Sexy dreams!
Scary dreams!

The kind that make you jump from bed until
you realize the monster wasn't real.
Or maybe the ones that make you wish you
weren't alone in your bed.

Finally, the descent into the deep, dark,
cavern of sleep, where you know nothing, hear
nothing, and time means nothing.

Continued on the next page

And then you awake!

That kind of sleep, that had you wrapped in
layers upon layers of thick, woolen blankets of darkness,
insulating you from the stimulus of the world of light,
must be like being dead.

Except for the waking part!

My Folks

When I was just a tot, and didn't know a lot, everything around me was big and loud and scary.
All the people I saw were giants, even our dog was huge and hairy, but the one thing I could count on, when I was too frightened or too sad, was the warm and loving arms of my mama and my dad, --- My Folks.

Then as I grew older and started going off to school, I knew that I was getting smarter and my parents were just old fools, but they'd put up with the dumb things I did, and chalked it up to me, just being a kid.

For a long time things weren't so good. I felt alone and mad and misunderstood. Got in trouble and kicked out of school, stole a bike and ran into the law, but even through this, they were there after all. --- My Folks

It took some time and doing but we got past those teenage years. Sometimes it was good sometimes bad, sometimes laughter, sometimes tears. I finally grew up and went out on my own, and started to find out about being alone, but deep down inside I knew if I had to I could always go home to my mom and my dad, too --- My Folks

Now, after several more years and a family of my own, it finally hit home, what parents are all about. It's being there and loving you, even when they'd like to kick you out. Through all the years of growing up and some grief that I'd caused them, whenever I had some problems, they were always there to help me solve them --- My Folks

Sometimes we don't know how good things are and we take our family for granted. They've always been there, and always will be, no matter how we treat them. But there comes a time as the years go by when age takes its toll and the ones who've loved you most won't be there anymore.

I watched my mom and dad age before my eyes, their bodies grow weaker, their steps grow slower and their memories unlike they were before. Then much too soon, one was gone then later on the other. Now all I have are the memories of my father and my mother --- My Folks.

Author's parents, Glenn and Flora Taylor wedding day, December 29th 1928

What Goes Around..........

Human babies,
what odd little creatures.
Mostly hairless and helpless
with similar features.

Their heads too large
and feet too small,
although they can cry
they can't talk at all.

Dependent on us
for all of their needs,
their every wish
to them we concede.

Toys or bugs
or anything else,
whatever they grasp
will go in their mouths.

What a joy it is
to watch them grow
and laugh out loud
when they suck on a toe.

We wipe their slobber
and clean their rears
with the knowledge
that in the coming years,

they may be doing
the same for us,
returning the favor
without any fuss.

It's said "once a man, twice a child."
We go through life
knowing all of the while
we're regressing back
to where we began.
Eventually our lives
will be in their hands..

End of The Line In Socorro

As the cowboy rode toward Socorro town,
he thought about the man he'd been hunting down,
this dirty outlaw that had murdered his wife.
He swore that soon he'd take the man's life.

The trail had been long, hard, dusty, and hot,
but he knew tomorrow he'd have his shot,
at this mangy dog he'd been trailing for months,
and in his heart he had a hunch,
after riding this far,
he'd find his man at the local bar.

Early next morning he rode into town,
gave a dollar to a boy to pass the word around,
he'd meet this skunk in the street at one,
and swore that's where he'd get the job done.

At one o'clock sharp the two came together
knowing only one man would come out the better.
But the killer had an ace up his sleeve..........

a friend with a rifle, who he believed,
would kill this cowboy with a shot from behind,
and end this threat for the very last time.

The killer drew first and the cowboy went down.
Luckily, just a graze in the arm,
but his fall made the rifleman miss,
and the cowboy rolled with his gun in his fist,
shot the man twice then turned to the other,
emptied his gun, but needn't have bothered.

His first shot hit the man square in the head.
When his body hit the ground
the killer was dead.

The death wouldn't heal the ache in his heart,
but the cowboy knew he'd have to make a new start.
Somehow, somewhere, he'd start a new life,
knowing it would be hard without his sweet wife.

Caught in the Middle

If you had it to do over
be one sibling of three
would you want to be oldest, youngest,
or the middle one like me?

There are perks that come
from being first in line.
The parents give all their attention
and all of their time.

Then number two comes along
and the attention is spread.
The novelty wears off
and the newness is dead.

Finally number three
enters their world.
By this time, they don't care
if it is a boy or a girl.

This one will always be
the baby of the three,
usually watched and protected
like the baby should be.

The oldest and youngest
in their own ways are
boss. And the one in the
middle sometimes gets
lost.

Turning Points

Do you ever think of the little things
that could've changed your life?
If you had taken a different turn,
a left instead of a right.

If you hadn't been fired from that job
and taken one that's new,
you wouldn't have met these people
who now mean so much to you.

Maybe you were late, missed a
flight, and the plane crashed in route.
If it hadn't have been for that delay
you could have been killed no doubt.

There are many little changes made,
looking back we can say,
that would have changed our lives
in very dramatic ways.

Call it fate or just blind luck
that led us to where we are,
but either way, we had as much control
as wishing on a star.

Lovely Wings

Of all the life here on this earth,
the tiny, large and tall,
meek and mild, dangerous and wild,
one of the most wonderful things of all,
is not the one that runs the fastest
or flies highest in the sky.
It's the one we all admire,
the lovely butterfly.

It doesn't bite, it doesn't sting
or seem to hurt a thing,
just floats gently here and there,
sometimes carried on the wind.

One of the few things on this earth
that causes nothing strife,
only bringing joy and beauty
throughout its' too short life.

There seems to be no limit
to the colors that they fly.
Put here for us to enjoy
the lovely butterfly.

Our Real Heroes

There's nothing braver than a man
who'll take his own life in his hand,
to rush into a burning house
and with all his strength
pull someone out.

Or one who braves raging waters
trying to save the lives of others.
People that he doesn't know,
but no less important, even so.

The soldier in the battlefield
risking his life, so we won't yield
our way of life and what we believe in
to tyrants and bullies, and their kind of kin.

Volunteers who give of their time
in the service of others in need of a dime,
who, with just a little help,
out of poverty and despair
might find their way out.

Our policeman, who, most of the time,
go in harm's way and put their lives on the line,
to come between us and those who would hurt,
rob, and kill, the worst of the worst.

These are the real heroes to admire,
not actors, or singers, or those who aspire
to play at sports and gain fortune and fame,
and by way of their prowess build a big name.

So let's give tribute to those men and women
whose courage and sacrifice so unselfishly given,
help others go on with their lives as before,
and in their own way, encourage others to do more.

Go Fish

Do you go fishing,
or just sit there wishing,
that you could go fishing?

Have lots of work
can't take the time.
Maybe tomorrow.
That'll be just fine.

This tomorrow comes.
That tomorrow goes.
Things stay the same.
Maybe next week, who knows?

Money comes in.
Money goes out.
Nothing much changes
and I've little doubt

that soon down the line
I'll be sitting here
wishing, that I had taken
the time to just do more
fishing.

Procreation In Gooseville: A Love Story

The giant gander gazed longingly at the gorgeous female goose grazing in the grass among a group of other geese. "What a great gaggle of goslings we could create if we could get together," he thought.

With a glint in his eye he gave her his best goose grin that produced a glow on her goose face that said, " Come and get it your grand gooseling."

So the giant gander and the gorgeous goose were grateful when they were gone from the rest of the goose group that couldn't gaze at them while they were grabbing, grasping and groping each other in a most un-goosely fashion.

After much grinning and gasping and grooming and gyrating the two gay but gaunt geese settled back to wait through the gestation period to see what they had begat.

After a goodly time, they were greeted with a grand group of gregarious, goofy, gabbling, gawky goslings of different genders.

They were greatly grateful to the god
of geese and genuflected to his goose-ness
in thankfulness for this grand gift
that had been generated from their genitals.
And giant gander, gorgeous goose, and their
growing gang of goslings, in their little goosedom,
lived happily ever after

The Person Within

Black is black
and white is white,
but in between are
shades of gray.

The same is true
throughout all life no
matter what some
choose to say.

Living beings are
complicated.
Nothing's carved in stone.
We always like things simple
but sometimes things go
wrong.

Somewhere in the process cells may change
and inside cause a fuss.
The person who's affected
might not be the same as us.

The one we see on the outside
might not be the same within.
They could be a different person
living in someone else's skin.

So think of this when you might hear
of the trials some go through.
If, but for fate, or maybe
luck, that person could be
you.

Tough Ole Birds

Outside my window
I happen to see
a flock of starlings
perched in a tree.

A gray, weary day.
Snow has come down.
A foot of the white
now covers the ground.

It makes me wonder
how can they feed?
How can they find
all the things that they need?

They don't have much
to keep out the weather,
no hair or fur
only some feathers.

It has to be hard
to be born a bird.
The dangers inherent
are so absurd.

Hawks and eagles
and other birds of prey.
Then there are hunters
to spoil the day.

All the trials and hardships
a bird must endure
are too many to mention,
that's to be sure.

It's amazing to see
after all they go through,
in some ways they're tougher
than me and you.

Kiss the Blarney Stone

Politician and priest begin with a 'p'
and they both want something
from you and me.
The priest wants a convert,
the politician your vote,
and they both count on one thing,
your trust and your hope.

Each of these knows
how the public to sway
and convince the masses
to get their own way.

The stores they tell may test your belief
and promises made they know they can't keep,
but if they're told often enough,
most will hesitate to call their bluff.

It seems, most want to be led
and will believe whatever is said.
They go with their emotions
and not with their head.

Politicians and priests will say, without laughter,
that only through them your life will be better.
Just give them your money and your faith.
You'll be rich soon, or in the hereafter.

We pay these people to tell us these things
I guess because of the comfort it brings.
We tend to take the easiest road.
It's harder to think than it is to be told.

Continued on the next page

Of these others I speak, of the two 'p's,
just people they are, like you and me,
I think just filled with the gift of blarney.
Not much different than a carnival carny.

They rant and rave, bluster and cajole,
make promise after promise, because they know,
some of the results can never be known
and the ones that fail will never be owned.

To me they're like two "p's" in a pod,
each of them, trying real hard
to convince us of things that can't be true,
and without a bit of proof they continue to woo.

A salesman told me once, indeed,
"People buy what they want, not what they need,
so if you, as the salesman, can create the desire
they'll find the need, and you'll have a buyer."

So remember these words, when you're told all the stories,
promises made of wealth and glory,
are your decisions made out of want, or need?
Just stop and consider before you proceed.

My Buddy, My Beer and My Boat

Two old buzzards
sitting in a boat
hoping not to catch a fish.

The beer is still
cold, stories yet to
be told, and pretzels
still in the dish.

It's so nice to be out
with no one about
just you and me
and the beer.

The weather is nice
the beer is on ice,
and no wife
to yell in my ear.

A way from the honey do's
and honey don'ts
the yes you wills
and the no I won'ts.

It's peaceful out here
my mind is so clear
and the beer tastes so
fine. I don't want to go
I'm getting a glow
I've got a fish.
Just cut off my line..

North to Alaska

As our ship comes to a stop, it slowly
begins to turn to give us our first look
at the huge wall of ice that is the
Hubbard glacier.

Like a gargantuan flow of white chocolate
it has moved for centuries down the
hills and out to sea, building layer upon
layer, to create this wonderful spectacle.

Beautiful blue streaks run through out,
and like a living creature it cracks
and pops as an old person with old joints.
At first thought: incredibly old, gigantic,
beautiful, indestructible.
But to the left another sight.
The barren, rolling hills of another long gone glacier,
as if a giant razor had cleaned off
every whisker, and not a trace of ice left.

While we watch, in awe and wonder,
huge pieces of ice break away and fall
with thunderous splashes into the water below,
to float away and begin
to slowly dissolve and become one
with the sea again.

Maybe this crystal giant isn't so
indestructible after all.
It's impervious to anything, except---- warmth.

The Wind and The Palm

The Fan Palm tree stood all alone with feet clinging desperately to the sandy soil mixed with the broken shards of thousands of long unused sea shells.

It was silhouetted against the clear, soft blue of the sky, with just a sprinkling of cottony clouds floating here and there to break up the monotony.

Then, a little breeze moved through the limbs that looked like long, thin arms with huge hands. At the end of each hand were more than two dozen slender tapered strands, like green witches fingers.

The wind thought to itself, "I will blow this tree to the ground."
And it blew harder and harder until the Palm, with its long, dangling fingers, were bending and thrashing about in a mad frenzy,
up and down, back and forth, waving frantically this way and that, fighting desperately against the invisible onslaught.

The wind blew and blew as hard as it was able that day,
but the palm retained its tenuous hold in the dry, barren, soil.

And the wind said, "You were the stronger one today. I am tired now, but I will come again soon,
and maybe next time I will be the stronger one."

Watermelon Boy

My father told me once, indeed, don't ever swallow a watermelon seed. Cause if you do, there's no doubt that little seed will begin to sprout. Then vines will grow, and they'll come out of your nose, your ears and mouth. And people will come from miles and miles to stare at the strange little watermelon child.

From that day on I tried and tried never to swallow a seed inside. But one time it couldn't be helped. One slipped on down. I let out a "yelp," ran to my mother, told her the story, said "I don't want to be a watermelon boy." She said "Don't listen to your father, don't believe what he said. By this time tomorrow, after a night in bed, that seed will have passed, on its way out, leaving it no time to sprout."

What a relief I felt, over whelming joy,
I don't have to be a watermelon boy.
But a lesson I learned that day,
take what my father has to say and listen with a little doubt.
It's not always true, what comes out.

Now Is The Time

The past is only memories.

The future, only illusions.

The present, only these moments now.

The question is how we use them?

It's A Different World Today

How I miss the simpler times
when I was growing up.
Softball in the school yard,
my first bike,
and playing with my pup.

We played soldiers in the field next door
with weeds stuck in our hair,
camouflaged like snipers
so no one could see us there.

I was Tarzan in the trees
in our big back yard,
swinging down on vines of rope,
sometimes landing hard.

Many hours spent at the river
with fishing pole or gun.
Hunting birds and rabbits
or just exploring in the sun.

Winter was a lot more fun back then
and I think that I should know.
We would grab on to the bumpers
of cars
and go off sliding in the snow.

Spending hours at the swimming pool
till I was wrinkled as a prune.
Eyes turned red from chlorine
thinking, "I'd better get out soon."

To me, this seems a lot more fun
than sitting on a couch
staring at a computer
till your eyes burn out.

Or pecking texts on a phone
a hundred times a day.
I know this is a whole new world
but me, I prefer the olden way

Sept. 11, 2001

Another Day in Infamy

September 11th, in New York city was a clear and beautiful day.
People went about their jobs. In the parks the children did play.
Old folks on benches were feeding the birds, everyone so blasé,
each in their own world, doing everyday things,
not knowing what was coming their way.

From a far-a-way land these men they arrived. With hate they
came to destroy. Their mission, to kill, to maim and frighten.
How many, they had no way of knowing.

Inspired by leaders who claimed to have knowledge of what their God wanted of
them, these men, without question,
followed their orders and set out to create mayhem.

On that fateful day they hijacked some planes and turned them on a new course.
Each of the four with a target in mind, to destroy with incredible force.

They first hit one building, then the other, filled with innocent workers. Men and
women, who had done them no harm.
Almost three thousand victims of murder.

Even as the buildings were collapsing to the ground, the brave police and firemen
came running, with debris still falling around. Risking life and limb they rushed
inside, hoping against hope, some may still be alive. But they themselves lost out that
day when the walls came tumbling down, and buried them in tons of rubble in the
middle of New York town.

The other planes crashed and many lives were lost but it could have been much,
much worse,
if it hadn't been for the heroes on board who fought them all the way to the earth.

We'll never forget that fateful day and the loved ones that were lost,
and the things that people do in the name of their God, and the terrible, terrible cost.

www.ingramcontent.com/pod-product-compliance
Lightning Source LLC
Chambersburg PA
CBHW052202110526
44591CB00012B/2044